Mel Bay Presents The Frank Vignola Jazz Se

120 2-bar ii-V Riffs

by Frank Vignola

1 2 3 4 5 6 7 8 9 0

Visit us on the Web at www.melbay.com — E-mail us at email@melbay.com

Contents

In this book you will find 120 two-bar ii-V7 riffs. There are ten different riffs for each of the twelve keys. Learn these riffs in all possible positions and using as many different fingerings as you can find. This will help you to learn the fingerboard and to find the best fingerings and position for you.

ii-V7 Phrases
Key of C Major

Frank Vignola

ii-V7 Phrases
Key of D♭ Major

Frank Vignola

ii-V7 Phrases
Key of D Major

Frank Vignola

ii-V7 Phrases

Key of E♭ Major

Frank Vignola

ii-V7 Phrases
Key of E Major

Frank Vignola

ii-V7 Phrases
Key of F Major

Frank Vignola

ii-V7 Phrases
Key of Gb Major

Frank Vignola

ii-V7 Phrases
Key of G Major

Frank Vignola

ii-V7 Phrases
Key of A♭ Major

Frank Vignola

ii-V7 Phrases

Key of A Major

Frank Vignola

ii-V7 Phrases
Key of B♭ Major

Frank Vignola

ii-V7 Phrases
Key of B Major

Frank Vignola